THE LEIPZIG
CONNECTION

A group of psychologists celebrating Wilhelm
Wundt's 80th birthday. Wundt is seated, center left.

Paolo Lionni

THE LEIPZIG CONNECTION

The Systematic Destruction
of American Education

Heron Books

Sheridan, Oregon

Published by Heron Books
20950 S.W. Rock Creek Road
Sheridan, Oregon 97378

ISBN: 0-89739-001-6

First Printing: October, 1980
Second Printing: August, 1981
Third Printing: November, 1988
Fourth Printing: January, 1993
Fifth Printing: January, 2013

Cover Design: Paolo Lionni
Front Cover Photo: Loren Leed

Printed in U.S.A.

Contents

Preface

Iɴ the final years of the 19th century, a great transformation began in American education. By the end of the first world war, Americans would notice increasingly a change in the way their children were being educated. In the succeeding decades, the same schools that once nurtured the American dream would become infested with drugs and crime, and high schools would be graduating students who could barely read, spell, or do simple arithmetic.

This report details the origins of a national metamorphosis, yet it is hardly definitive. Major changes in American education, along the same lines as those described herein (and, in many cases, overlapping them), were wrought by the great Carnegie and Ford "philanthropies" and by a host of individuals (*i.e.*, Col. Parker, Goddard, Terman, Yerkes, Binet, Piaget, Watson, Skinner, Freire, Illich, *et al.*). Agencies other than those mentioned in the book also played major roles. Foremost among these undoubtedly is the august and hyperactive NEA with its National Training Labs, publisher of the *Journal of Applied Behavioral Science*. Special mention should also be made of UNESCO's International Bureau of Education (formerly the Institut Jean-Jacques Rousseau), born in 1925 of a generous grant from the Rockefeller Foundation.

These initial and somewhat unexpected findings, however incomplete, are released in order to help others analyze more clearly this tragic transformation of the national character. Further research has simply substantiated and enlarged upon the thesis of this work.

The ongoing debasement of philosophy and ethics, and its social consequences, is a tangled tale and, where references are not pursued or fully detailed, it is not because of an unwillingness to answer the questions raised rather is it from a desire to suggest a broader context within which the story unfolds. Those who contend, with Wilhelm Wundt, that history and its processes are responsible for the formation of individuals and their views (rather than the reverse) will undoubtedly find this approach unpalatable; then again, not everyone would want this tale untangled.

1. A New Domain

WILHELM Maximilian Wundt was born in 1832 in Neckarau, a small town in southern Germany.[1] Wundt entered the university at Tubingen when he was 19, transferred to Heidelberg after half a year, and graduated as a medical doctor from that university in 1856. He stayed on at Heidelberg for the next seventeen years, working first as a professor's assistant, and later as a professor himself, in the field of psychology. Psychology, at that time, meant simply the study (ology) of the soul (psyche), or mind.[2]

---

1. Perhaps the best descriptive biography of Wundt is contained in Professor Edwin G. Boring's *A History of Experimental Psychology*, 2nd ed. (New York: Appleton-Century-Crofts, Inc., 1929). See, also, Schultz, Duane P., *A History of Modern Psychology* (New York: Academic Press, 1969), and Murphy, Gardner and Joseph K. Kovach, *Historical Introduction to Modern Psychology*, 6th ed. (New York Harcourt Brace, 1972), for excellent overviews of the development of experimental psychology.

2. See, for example, *A Standard Dictionary of the English Language* (New York: Funk & Wagnalls Co., 1895), which notes the intrusion of the new German definition of the word in a reference note inserted by Wundt's student James Mark Baldwin.

In 1874, Wundt left Heidelberg to take a position as professor of philosophy at Zurich. He stayed there for only a year, and then accepted a chair in philosophy at the University of Leipzig, in Germany. He was to remain at Leipzig for the rest of his academic career, eventually being appointed rector of the university. Wundt died in 1920.

Those are some of the vital statistics. What they omit is that Wundt was the founder of experimental psychology and the force behind its dissemination throughout the western world.

To Wundt, a thing made sense and was worth pursuing if it could be measured, quantified, and scientifically demonstrated. Seeing no way to do this with the human soul, he proposed that psychology concern itself solely with experience. As Wundt put it:

> ...it truly appears to be a useless waste of energy to keep returning to such aimless discussions about the nature of the psyche, which were in vogue for a while, and practically still are, instead, rather, of applying one's energies where they will produce real results.[3]

3. Shipley, Thorne, ed., *Classics in Psychology* (New York: Philosophical Library, 1961), 52-3, extracted from Wundt, Wilhelm, *Contributions to the Theory of Sensory Perception*, trans. from *Beitrage zur Theorie der Sinneswahrnehmung* (Leipzig: C.F. Winter, 1862).

Germany was the center of civilization: its scientific and technological advances were well-known. The Germans excelled in the application of scientific terms and procedures to previously non-scientific areas. Hegel, at the University of Berlin, had proposed to make of history a scientific subject; he became Germany's leading philosopher, emulated by a generation of students. Karl Marx injected Hegel's theories with economics and sociology, developing a "philosophy" of "dialectical materialism." Herbart and Fechner applied mathematical principles to learning[4]; Muller and Helmholtz grafted physiology to behavior; Fritsch and Hitzig applied electrical stimulation to the brain to determine the relationship of brain functions to behavior. Throughout the revolutions and revolts of 1848 across Europe, the rise of the Socialist Internationals, and the forced unification of the new Germany by Otto von Bismarck, Germany was a flourishing center of culture and the sciences,

---

4. Herbart and Fechner are perhaps the direct lineal antecedents of Wundt in the area of education. See Boring, *op. cit.*, 250-260 and 275-296. Herbart's psychology, as it applies in particular to education, is lucidly described in Paul Monroe's *A Brief Course in the History of Education* (New York: Macmillan, 1927). See also Dunkel, Harold B., *Herbart & Education* (New York: Random House, 1969) and DeGarmo, Charles, Herbart and the Herbartians (New York: Charles Scribner's Sons, 1912), for good discussions of the impact of Herbart's views on education.

each of its universities a magnet for the ambitious intellectual youth of Europe and the United States. Leipzig was no exception and one of its principal attractions was Wundt, who was attempting to place his ideas within the mainstream of German scientism by redefining psychology as a physiological rather than a philosophical subject.

Soon after his arrival at Leipzig in 1875, he had established the world's first psychological laboratory. Initially small and primitive, it soon increased to eleven rooms. He supplemented his new laboratory with a journal, Philosophical Studies, which became the official organ of both the new laboratory and the newly redefined "science" of psychology. Wundt stated his overall intention in clear terms:

> *The work which I here present to the public is an attempt to mark out a new domain of science.*[5]

Wundt's basic approach was to gather data concerning physiological responses in order to clarify how the individual experienced feelings and sensations. He was convinced that perceptions and experiences could be understood through measurable physiological reactions.

5. Schultz, *op.cit.*, 45

Wundt noticed that reactions began with stimulation, followed by (1) perception, in which the experience exists within the individual; (2) "apperception," in which the body (or so he thought) identifies the stimulus and combines it with other stimuli, and (3) an act of will which results in (4) a reaction to the stimulus. What was will? For Wundt, will was the direct result of the combination of perceived stimuli, not an independent, individual intention as psychology and philosophy had, with some notable exceptions, held up to that time.[6]

It seems, at times, that Wundt was the kind of person who is particularly likely to be underestimated. His personality was not sufficiently picturesque to make him stand out on that account; and his work shows no single, brilliant contribution to knowledge that can be readily circumscribed and labeled with a phrase.

6. Here, Wundt was condensing and organizing the work of his contemporaries, with primary emphasis on the works of Herbart. Psychologist R.I. Watson, in *The Great Psychologists* (Philadelphia: Lippincott, 1963), p. 257, describes Wundt as a:

    ... great synthesizer of research findings, both of the work that preceded him and of that carried on by his students. Wundt's forte was not luminous ideas lighting upon the dark corners or giving us a new dazzling perspective on the old picture. Rather, he worked over a thousand details, cleaning here, repairing there, filling a crack here, so that psychology leaving his hands was an improved, more coherent picture, but still a familiar one.

*His great achievement was the bringing into
effective relations of many things which, it is
true, had existed before, but which had not been
integrated into an effective organization; and
somehow human beings are prone to regard
such achievements as less striking and less
creative than those of the order of Helmholtz's
and Fechner's. But the man who sensed the
movements of scientific thought as Wundt did,
who embodied them in the first laboratory, who
gave them form in an influential system, and
who imparted them to enthusiastic students
who were proud to carry on his work, has no
small claim to the title often accorded him, that
of father of modern psychology. Wundt himself was not unaware of the debt psychology
owed him, and not altogether indifferent as to
whether or not it was recognized. In his role as
father, he inclined toward the patriarchal,
almost toward the papal; he reserved the
right to speak with authority, to pronounce ex
cathedra on psychology and psychologists,
and to draw a distinct line of demarcation
between authentic psychology and psychology of which he did not approve. Even to-day,
so great have been his influence and prestige,
the term "experimental psychology" to many
still has as its first connotation the kind of*

psychology which was taught in Wundt's laboratory or which Wundt recognized and approved. [7]

Wundt made two major contributions to the transformation of education in the West. The first was theoretical and will be taken up here. The second is addressed in the next chapter, "The Impress."

Wundt asserted that man is devoid of spirit and self-determinism. He set out to prove that man is the summation of his experiences, of the stimuli which intrude upon his consciousness and unconsciousness. In directing the work of his students, he focused their energies on minute examinations of sensory perceptions, in an attempt to dissect and quantify every aspect of action and reaction. What determined the difference between one individual and another in reaction time to stimuli? Why do some individuals combine stimuli differently than do others? What are the "laws" of the associations that can be formed between words? Wundt and his students regarded such questions as paramount.[8]

7.　Heidbreder, Edna, *Seven Psychologies* (New York: D. Appleton-Century Company, Inc., 1933), 96-7.

8.　Boring, *op. cit.*, 339-344.

A highly respected physiologist, Wundt established the new psychology as a study of the brain and the central nervous system. From Wundt's work, it was only a short step to the later redefinition of the meaning of education. Originally, education meant the drawing out of a person's innate talents and abilities[9] by imparting the knowledge of languages, scientific reasoning, history, literature, rhetoric, etc.—the channels through which those abilities would flourish and serve. To the experimental psychologist, however, education became the process of exposing the student to "meaningful" experiences so as to ensure desired reactions:

> ... *learning is the result of modifiability in the paths of neural conduction. Explanations of even such forms of learning as abstraction and generalization demand of the neurones only growth, excitability, conductivity, and modifiability. The mind is the connection-system of man; and learning is the process of connecting. The situation-response formula is adequate to cover learning of any sort, and the really influential factors in learning are readiness of*

9. A concept going back to the Latin root of the word, *eductus*, to bring out, lead forth, from *e*, out of, + *ducere*, lead. Hence, "to develop the faculties and powers of by teaching, instruction, or schooling," from Emery, H.G., and K.G. Brewster, *The New Century Dictionary of the English Language* (New York: Appleton·Century-Crofts, 1927).

> *the neurones, sequence in time, belongingness, and satisfying consequences.* [10]

If one assumes (as did Wundt) that there is nothing there to begin with but a body, a brain, and a nervous system, then one must try to educate by inducing sensations in that nervous system. Through these experiences, the individual will learn to respond to any given stimulus, with the "correct" response. The child is not, for example, thought capable of volitional control over his actions, or of deciding whether he will act or not act in a certain way: his actions are thought to be preconditioned and beyond his control, because he is a stimulus-response mechanism. According to this thinking, he *is* his reactions. Wundt's thesis laid the philosophical basis for the principles of conditioning later developed by Pavlov (who studied physiology in Leipzig, in 1884, five years after Wundt had inaugurated his laboratory there) and American behavioral psychologists such as Watson and Skinner; for lobotomies and electro-convulsive therapy; for schools oriented more toward the socialization of the child than toward the development of intellect; and for the emergence of a society more and more blatantly devoted to the gratification of sensory desires at the expense of responsibility and achievement.

10. Pintner, Rudolph, *et al., An Outline of Educational Psychology*, rev. ed. (New York: Barnes & Noble, 1934), 79.

2. The Impress

WUNDT'S second major contribution to psychology's preempting of education wasn't theoretical at all: he produced the first generation of researchers, professors, and publicists in the new psychology. This group went on to establish experimental psychology throughout Europe and the United States:

> *Through these students, the Leipzig Laboratory exercised an immense influence on the development of psychology. It served as the model for the many new laboratories that were developed in the latter part of the nineteenth century. The many students who flocked to Leipzig, united as they were in point of view and common purpose, constituted a school of thought in psychology.*[1]

1. Schultz, *op. cit.*, 45.

The list of Wundt's students is a *Who's Who* of early European and American psychologists. In succeeding years, one could go to almost any major European or American university and study the new psychology with a professor who had received his Ph.D. directly from Wundt at Leipzig.[2]

Naturally Leipzig became the Mecca of students who wished to study the "new" psychology–a psychology that was no longer a branch of speculative philosophy, no longer a fragment of the science of physiology, but a novel and daring and exciting attempt to study mental processes by the experimental and quantitative methods common to all science. For the psychology of Leipzig was, in the eighties and nineties, the newest thing under the sun. It was the psychology for bold young radicals who believed that the ways of the mind could be measured and treated experimentally–and who possibly thought of themselves, in their private reflections, as pioneers on the newest frontier of science, pushing its method into reaches of

---

2. Some of the more notable of Wundt's European students were Kiesow at Turin, Kirschmann at Toronto and later Leipzig, Storring at Zurich and Bonn, Kulpe and Kraepelin ("father" of schizophrenia) at Munich, Meumann at Hamburg, Marbe at Wurzburg, Lehmann at Copenhagen, Wirth and Krueger at Leipzig, Lipps at Zurich, Durr at Bern, and Lange at Tubingen. Boring, *op. cit.*, 427-9.

experience that it had never before invaded. At any rate they threw themselves into their tasks with industry and zest. They became trained introspectionists and, adding introspection to the resources of the physiological laboratories, they attempted the minute analysis of sensation and perception. They measured reaction-times, following their problems into numerous and widespread ramifications. They investigated verbal reactions, thus extending their researches into the field of association. They measured the span and the fluctuations of attention and noted some of its more complex features in the "complication experiment," a laboratory method patterned after the situation that gave rise to the astronomer's problem of the "personal equation." In their studies of feeling and emotion they recorded pulse-rates, breathing rates, and fluctuations in muscular strength, and in the same connection they developed methods of recording systematically and treating statistically the impressions observed by introspection. They also developed the psychophysical methods and in addition made constant use of resources of the physiological laboratory. And throughout all their endeavors they were dominated by the conception of a psychology that should be scientific as opposed to speculative; always they attempted to rely on exact observation, experimentation, and measurement. Finally when they left Leipzig and worked in laboratories of their own–chiefly in American or German universities–most of them retained enough of the Leipzig impress to teach a psychology that, whatever the subsequent development of the individual's thought, bore traces of the system which was recognized at Leipzig as orthodox.[3]

The young Americans who studied with Wundt returned to found departments of psychology throughout the United States. With the prestige attached to having studied in Germany, these men found little difficulty in securing positions of influence at major American universities. Each became successful to a marked degree; each trained scores, often hundreds, of Ph.D. students in psychology; each contributed to new associations and publications in the new field of study. Almost without exception, every one of them became involved in another field which lay open to the advance of German psychology–the field of education.

The first of Wundt's American students to return to the United States was G. Stanley Hall. Returning from Leipzig in 1883, he joined the

---

3.   Heidbreder, *op. cit.*, 94-5.

faculty of Baltimore's new Johns Hopkins University, which was being established after the model of the great German universities. Hall organized the psychology laboratory at Johns Hopkins and, in 1887, established the American Journal of Psychology, giving the "adherents of the new psychology not only a storehouse for contributions both experimental and theoretical, but a sense of solidarity and independence."[4]

Two years later, in 1889, when Clark University was established in Worcester, Massachusetts, Hall was chosen to be its first president. In 1892 he played a leading role in founding the American Psychological Association. Hall became known for his intensive studies of child development (which directly fostered the child study movement in this country) and in 1904 he published his masterwork, the two-volume Adolescence: Its Psychology and Its Relations to Physiology, Anthropology, Sociology, Sex, Crime, Religion, and Education,[5] welding experimental psychology to child education.

Hall was also instrumental in furthering the career of a man who was to have an unusually profound effect on the course of American education: John Dewey. Dewey was born in Vermont,

4. Murphy and Kovach, *op. cit.*, 175.

5. Schultz, *op. cit.*, 175.

graduated from the University of Vermont, spent a little over two years teaching high school, and enrolled as a graduate student at Johns Hopkins University[6] (following in the footsteps of his older brother by 1½ years, Davis Rich Dewey, who later became professor of economics and statistics at M.I.T. and who was, for 29 years, managing editor of the *American Economic Review*). He spent a year studying under Hall, and received his doctorate from Johns Hopkins in 1884. He taught for ten years at the universities of Michigan and Minnesota and in 1886 (the same year the National Education Association was formed), while a professor at Michigan, Dewey published *Psychology*, the first American textbook on the revised subject. In late 1895 he was invited to join the faculty of the Rockefeller-endowed University of Chicago as head of the departments of philosophy, psychology, and pedagogy (teaching). That same year, the University allocated $1,000 to establish an education laboratory in which Dewey could apply psychological principles and experimental techniques

6. There have been many accounts of Dewey's influence on education in the United States. For his role in the "Chicago School" of psychology see Schutz, *op. cit.*, 124-6. See also Arthur G. Wirth's *John Dewey as Educator: His Design for Work in Education (1894-1904)*, (New York: John Wiley & Sons, Inc., 1966); Baker, Melvin, *Foundations of John Dewey's Educational Theory* (New York: King's Crown Press, 1955); and Bernstein, Richard J., *John Dewey* (New York: Washington Square, 1966).

G. Stanley Hall, Wundt's first American student and John Dewey's mentor. *Clark University Archives*

John Dewey: "The ultimate problem of all education is to coordinate the psychological and social factors..."
Courtesy of University of Minnesota Archives.

Edward Lee Thorndike: "Subjects such as arithmetic, language, and history include content that is intrinsically of little value." *Harvard University Archive.*

A typical installation modelled after Wundt's Leipzig facility; in this case the main psychological laboratory at Clark University, at the turn of the century.
Clark University Archives.

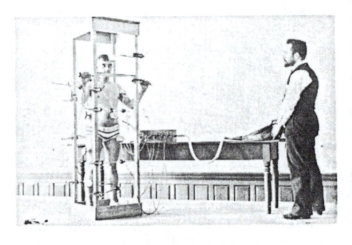

Experimental psychology at work–the backdrop for today's educational methods. *Clark University Archives.*

to the study of learning. The laboratory opened in January, 1896, as the Dewey School, later to become known as the Laboratory School of the University of Chicago.

For Dewey, the school was a place "where his theories of education could be put into practice, tested, and scientifically evaluated."[7]

...Dewey...sought to apply the doctrines of experience and experiment to everyday life and, hence, to education...seeking via this model institution to pave the way for the 'schools of the future.' There he had put into actual practice three of the revolutionary beliefs he had culled from the new psychology: that to put the child in possession of his fullest talents, education should be active rather than passive; that to prepare the child for a democratic society, the school should be social *rather than individualist; and that to enable the child to think* creatively, *experimentation rather than imitation should be encouraged.*[8] [emphasis added]

7. DePencier, Ida B., *The History of the Laboratory Schools, The University of Chicago, 1896-1965* (Chicago: Quadrangle Books, 1967), 13. Another pro-Dewey account, more oriented to Dewey's philosophy of education, is G. Max Wingo's *The Philosophy of American Education* (Lexington: D.C. Heath, 1965)

8. Cremin, Lawrence A., David A. Shannon, and Mary Evelyn Townsend, *A History of Teachers College, Columbia University* (New York: Colum-

This was a sharp break from the traditional definition of education. In Dewey's own words:

> *Education consists either in the ability to use one's powers in a social direction, or else in ability to share in the experiences of others and thus widen the individual consciousness to that of the race*[9]*...The ultimate problem of all education is to coordinate the psychological and social factors...The coordination demands...that the child be capable of expressing himself, but in such a way as to realize social ends.*[10]

Although today Dewey's views are in practice in the great majority of American schools, before the turn of the century they were revolutionary. The Wundtian redefinition of "education" to mean feeding experiential data to a young brain and nervous system, rather than the teaching of mental skills, led to the abdication of the traditional role

bia University Press, 1954), 45 . Although a strongly flattering "official" history of Teachers College, this book is nonetheless a storehouse of data pertinent to the invasion of psychology into American education.

9. Dewey, John, *Lectures for the First Course in Pedagogy*, unpublished, No. 1 (1896), 1; quoted in Wirth, *op. cit.*, 28.

10. Dewey, John, *Plan of Organization of the University Primary School*, unpublished, University of Chicago, 1895 (?) ; quoted in Wirth, *op. cit.*, 88.

of the teacher as educator. Its place was taken by the concept of the teacher as a guide in the socialization of the child, leading each youngster to *adapt* to the specific *behavior* required of him in order for him to *get along* in his group.[11] Dewey called for a levelling of individual differences into a common pool of students who are the object of learning technicians devising the social order of the future. [12]

According to professors Mort and Vincent of Columbia Teachers College, "John Dewey was the culminating theorist in three centuries of educational writing."[13] To Dewey, as to Wundt, man was an animal, alone with his reactions and entirely dependent upon experiential data. He believed

11. See, in particular, John Dewey's *My Pedagogic Creed*, in which he states:

> *The school is primarily a social institution. Education being a social process, the school is simply that form of community life in which all those agencies are concentrated that will be most effective in bringing the child to share in the inherited resources of the race, and to use his own powers for social ends.*

Quoted in Mayer, Frederick, ed., *Foundations of Contemporary Education* (New Haven: College & University Press, 1966), 139.

12. Dewey contended that the public schools must "take an active part in determining the social order of the future...according as the teachers align themselves with the newer forces making for social control of economic forces." Quoted in Allen, Gary, "Hands off our Children!," *American Opinion*, XVIII, No. 9 (October, 1975), 3.

13. Mort, Paul R., and William S. Vincent, *Introduction to American Education* (New York: McGraw-Hill, 1954), 43.

that learning occurred only through experience, that the stimulus-response mechanism was basic to learning, and that teachers were not instructors, but designers of learning experiences.[14] At the Dewey School in Chicago, and later at Teachers College of Columbia University, Dewey was able to implement and promote the interchangeability of psychology and education, successfully enough to become the leading figure in American education. Yet Dewey, the "Father of American Education," was only one of the practitioners of Wundt's revised psychology who critically transformed American education and, consequently, American life.

---

14. *Ibid.*, 44, and Wirth, *op. cit.*, 78-80.

3. Positioning

WHILE G. Stanley Hall had been Wundt's first American student, his compatriot James McKeen Cattell had the distinction of being Wundt's first assistant and, later, the most effective publicist and promoter of the revised psychology.

Cattell was born in 1860 in Pennsylvania, and received his bachelor's degree from Lafayette College (where his father was president) in 1880. He then spent a short period of time in Germany, where he met Wundt and saw his laboratory. Returning to Germany in 1883, Cattell went to Leipzig and told Wundt that he was going to be his assistant. Wundt acceded and Cattell spent the next three years experimenting in Wundt's lab, receiving his Ph.D. from him in 1886. Cattell's primary interests lay in mental testing and in individual differences in ability.[1]

---

1. Murphy and Kovach, *op. cit.*, 169-72, and Schultz, *op. cit.*, 117-22.

One series of experiments Cattell performed while at Leipzig examined the manner in which a person sees the words he is reading. Testing adults who knew how to read, Cattell found they could recognize words without having to sound out the letters. From this, he reasoned that words are not read by compounding the letters, but are perceived as "total word pictures." He determined that little is gained by teaching the child his sounds and letters as the first step to being able to read. Since they could recognize words very rapidly, the way to teach children how to read would be to show them words, and tell them what the words were. This breakthrough of Cattell's led to the adoption of a sight-reading method in many schools and school systems throughout the United States. Its failure to produce an expected increase in literacy is hardly attributable to Cattell's perception or find-ings, which have been validated and enlarged upon in our time with superb results by Glenn Doman, of The Institutes for the Achievement of Human Potential.[2] Rather, Cattell's results were subse-quently applied by teachers trained in the new psychology, who managed to convert even this

2. For more information on Doman's work, see his books: *What To Do About Your Brain Injured Child*, Doubleday, 1974, *How to Teach Your Baby to Read*, Doubleday, 1975 (over one million copies sold), and *Teach Your Baby Math*, Simon and Schuster, 1979.

otherwise brilliant observation into a national crisis.

Returning to the United States, Cattell lectured at Bryn Mawr and at the University of Pennsylvania for a year. In 1887 (the same year in which Hall published his *Aspects of German Culture*), he left the country again to lecture at Cambridge, where he met and was deeply impressed by Charles Darwin's cousin, the English psychologist Francis Galton. Galton's theories held that "a man's natural abilities are derived by inheritance, under exactly the same limitations as are the form and physical features of the whole organic world."[3] Cattell quickly absorbed Galton's approach to eugenics, selective breeding, and the measurement of intelligence. Cattell was later to become the American leader in psychological testing, and in 1894 would administer the first battery of psychological tests ever given to a large group of people, testing the freshman and senior classes at Columbia University.

Returning from Cambridge, Cattell became professor of psychology at the University of Pennsylvania–the first professor of the revised subject anywhere in the world (Wundt's title was in philosophy). At Pennsylvania, he established one of the

3. Pintner, *op. cit.*, 14.

first psychological laboratories in the country, patterning it after Wundt's Leipzig model. Leaving Pennsylvania in 1891, Cattell joined the faculty of Columbia University as professor of psychology and head of Columbia's new psychology department, a critical position for the union of psychology and education.

At Columbia, Cattell shone as an organizer and publicist. To promote the new "science" of experimental psychology Cattell created publications which would carry the new subject to educators and scientists across the country. First he began a new journal, in 1894, called *The Psychological Review*. Then he purchased from Alexander Graham Bell the weekly publication *Science*, which later became the official journal of the American Association for the Advancement of Science. In 1900 he began *Popular Science Monthly,* continuing to publish it after 1915 as *Scientific Monthly*; that same year he began yet another publication, the weekly *School and Society*.[4] He also began a series of well-known reference works: *American Men of Science*, *Leaders in Education*, and *The Directory of American Scholars*; with publications such as these, he positioned the revised psychology within the mainstream of American thinking,

4.   Schultz, *op. cit.*, 119.

the proponents of this new field taking their places alongside our leading scientists, educators, and scholars in the pages of these reference books.

During his twenty-five years at Columbia, Cattell supervised 344 successful doctoral candidates in psychology. In 1895 he was elected president of the American Psychological Association, and in 1900 he became the first psychologist elected to the National Academy of Sciences. Although he never wrote a textbook, and was the author of only a few papers in his field, he publicized experimental psychology broadly, organized his colleagues, and promoted their accomplishments, enabling them to consolidate their positions in the departments of philosophy (and, later, psychology) at major universities across the country.[5]

A few of those colleagues deserve passing mention here as they directly influenced the fusion of experimental psychology and American education. James Mark Baldwin, who studied with Wundt, became a professor of psychology at Princeton in 1893, and in 1903 joined the psychology department at Johns Hopkins University. Baldwin was to become one of the leaders of American experimental psychology and editor of Cattell's *Psychological Review*. Andrew C. Armstrong, professor

5. Boring, *op. cit.*, 532-40.

of psychology at Wesleyan University, in building up Wesleyan's faculty in the revised subject,
hired (in 1896) his own former student, "the ardent
young experimentalist, Charles Judd, fresh from
Germany with a Leipzig doctorate from Wundt."[6]
Judd later left Wesleyan to become, successively,
instructor in psychology at New York University's
School of Pedagogy, professor of psychology and
pedagogy at the University of Cincinnati, director
of the psychological laboratory and psychology
instructor at Yale, and finally, in 1909, director
of the School of Education at the University of
Chicago.[7]

James Earl Russell, a student of Wundt's who
received his doctorate from Leipzig in 1894, came
to Columbia University in October, 1897, five
years after the New York College for the Training
of Teachers had received its permanent charter as
Columbia's Teachers College. Russell had already
occupied positions of administrative responsibility
having been, while at Leipzig, an official European
Agent for the Federal Bureau of Education (then
located in the Department of the Interior). Appointed head of the department of psychology and

6. Joncich, Geraldine, *The Sane Positivist: A Biography of Edward L. Thorndike* (Middletown: Wesleyan University Press, 1968), 73.

7. See the explicit reference in the *Encyclopaedia Britannica*, 15th ed., *Micropaedia*, Vol. V (Chicago: Encyclopaedia Britannica, 1976), 625.

general method, Russell directed the central department at Teachers College. That same year, Russell became dean of the College. He would run it for the next thirty years, building the largest institution in the world for the training of teachers.[8]

Thus, in 1897, the stage was about to be set for the propagation of Wundt's laboratory psychology throughout American education.

8.   Cremin, et al., *op. cit.*, 25-9.

4. Mice and Monkeys

WORKING closely with Cattell, Russell began to hire a faculty. One of his first choices was Frank McMurry, who had also studied psychology at Leipzig:

Active in the National Educational Association and in the National Society for the Scientific Study of Education, of which his brother Charles McMurry was the executive secretary, he (Frank) soon attracted the attention of James Russell. The result was that in the fall of 1898 he joined the Teachers College Faculty... His own studies of the principles of method [of John Dewey, ed.] emerged in 1907 in his book How to Study *and* Teaching How to Study, *followed by many additional treatments of the same theme. His basic interests also extended to the curriculum of the elementary school; his teaching and writing in this realm*

quickly established him as a pioneer of modern
progressive educational theory.[1]

It was the hiring by Russell of another practi-
tioner of the new fad, however, that was to result
in Columbia's becoming the connection for a fatal
dose of Wundtian psychology into the mainline of
American education. Edward Lee Thorndike was
trained in the new psychology by the first generation of Wundt's protégés. He graduated from Wesleyan University in 1895, after having studied with
Wundtians Armstrong and Judd. He went to graduate school at Harvard, studying under psychologist
William James, a transitional figure whose later
influence depended, to a substantial extent, on
his subtle furthering of physiological psychology
(under the guise of Pragmatism). While at Harvard,
Thorndike surprised James by doing research with
chickens, testing their behavior and pioneering
what later became known as "animal psychology":

As briefly stated by Thorndike himself, psy-
chology was the science of the intellect, char-
acter, and behavior of animals, including man.[2]

1. Cremin, *et al., op. cit.*, 46-7.

2. *Ibid.*, 44.

Thorndike applied for a fellowship at Columbia, was accepted by Cattell, and moved with his two most intelligent chickens to New York, where he continued his research and earned his Ph.D. in 1898.[3] Thorndike's specialty was the "puzzle box," into which he would put various animals (chickens, rats, cats) and let them find their way out by themselves. His doctoral dissertation on cats has become part of the classical literature of psychology.

After receiving his doctorate, he spent a year as a teacher of education at Western Reserve University, and it wasn't long before Cattell advised Dean Russell to visit Thorndike's first classroom at Western Reserve:

Although the Dean found him 'dealing with the investigations of mice and monkeys,' he came away 'satisfied that he was worth trying out on humans.' [4]

Russell offered Thorndike a job at Teachers College, where the experimenter remained for the next thirty years.

---

3. Schultz, *op. cit.*, 165.

4. Cremin, *et al.*, *op. cit.*, 43.

Thorndike was the first psychologist to study animal behavior in an experimental psychology laboratory and (following Cattell's suggestion) apply the same techniques to children and youths; as one result, in 1903, he published the book *Educational Psychology*. In the following years he published a total of 507 books, monographs, and articles.

Thorndike's primary assumption was the same as Wundt's: that man is an animal, that his actions are actually always reactions, and that he can be studied in the laboratory in much the same way as an animal might be studied. Thorndike equated children with the rats, monkeys, fish, cats, and chickens upon which he experimented in his laboratory and was prepared to apply what he found there to learning in the classroom. He extrapolated "laws" from his research into animal behavior which he then applied to the training of teachers, who took what they had learned to every corner of the United States and ran their classrooms, curricula, and schools on the basis of this new "educational" psychology.

In *The Principles of Teaching Based on Psychology* (1906), Thorndike proposed making "the study of teaching scientific and practical." This is his definition of the art of teaching:

...the art of giving and withholding stimuli with the result of producing or preventing certain responses. In this definition the term stimulus is used widely for any event which influences a person,—for a word spoken to him, a look, a sentence which he reads, the air he breathes, etc., etc. The term response is used for any reaction made by him,—a new thought, a feeling of interest, a bodily act, any mental or bodily condition resulting from the stimulus. The aim of the teacher is to produce desirable and prevent undesirable changes in human beings by producing and preventing certain responses. The means at the disposal of the teacher are the stimuli which can be brought to bear upon the pupil,–the teacher's words, gestures, and appearance, the condition and appliances of the school room, the books to be used and objects to be seen, and so on through a long list of the things and events which the teacher can control.[5]

These are the origins of conditioning and the later work of behavioral psychologists such as Watson (who received his Ph.D. from Dewey at

---

5. Thorndike, Edward L., *The Principles of Teaching Based on Psychology*, 1906 (New York: A.G. Seiler, 1925), 7-8. See also Thorndike, Edward L., *The Elements of Psychology*, 2nd ed. (New York: A.G. Seiler, 1915).

the University of Chicago in 1903 with a thesis entitled "Animal Education") and Skinner. Thorndike based conditioning on what he called the "law of effect," which held that those actions and behaviors leading to satisfaction would be impressed, or stamped in, on the child, and those leading to unsatisfactory results would be stamped out. Thus the only way to strengthen a child's "good" response is by reinforcing it, and the only way to eliminate a child's "bad" response is by denying it.

This theory creates certain problems for the educator. Should the child, for example, not want to learn his multiplication, the teacher will have to find some way of making multiplication pleasurable and rewarding, or the child just won't learn it. Similarly, if the child enjoys tossing pencils at his classmates, he will have to be instructed, by denying him pleasure, that such a "behavior" isn't permissible. This thinking favors a society which operates more on the basis of gratification than on the basis of reason or responsibility. Children expect to receive what is pleasurable, and what they desire, because they have learned in school that what is pleasurable is good, and what isn't pleasurable, isn't good. This is an inheritance from the stimulus-response teaching developed by Thorndike and transmitted to hundreds of thousands of teachers through the medium of "educational" psychology. Previously, of course, good behavior was considered its own reward; the idea of rewarding a child for behaving like a human being would only occur to someone who supposes that the child is basically an animal and would have seemed like an open invitation to blackmail to any sensible 19th-century parent.

What was the purpose of education, according to Thorndike?

> *Education is interested primarily in the general interrelation of man and his environment, in all the changes which make possible a better adjustment of human nature to its surroundings.*[6]

This is also the view of Dewey and other Wundtians—that man is a social animal who must learn to adapt to his environment, instead of learning how to ethically adapt the environment to suit his needs and those of society. Individualism and the developing of individual abilities give way to social conformity and adaptation; the product of education becomes "well-adjusted" (conditioned) children.

6. *Ibid.*, 3.

Thorndike also had specific views about education in the basics—the 3R's:

> *Studies of the capacities and interests of young children indicate the advisability of placing little emphasis before the age of six upon either the acquisition of those intellectual resources known as the formal tools—reading, spelling, arithmetic, writing, etc.—or upon abstract intellectual analysis.*[7]

> *Despite rapid progress in the right direction, the program of the average elementary school is too narrow and academic in character. Traditionally the elementary school has been primarily devoted to teaching the fundamental subjects, the three R 's, and closely related disciplines... Artificial exercises, like drills on phonetics, multiplication tables, and formal writing movements, are used to a wasteful degree. Subjects such as arithmetic, language, and history include content that is intrinsically of little value. Nearly every subject is enlarged unwisely to satisfy the academic ideal of thoroughness. That the typical school overempha-*

7. Thorndike, Edward L., and Arthur I. Gates, *Elementary Principles of Education* (New York: Macmillan, 1929), 308.

sizes instruction in these formal, academic skills as a means of fostering intellectual resources...is a justifiable criticism... Elimination of unessentials by scientific study, then, is one step in improving the curriculum.[8]

Thorndike was joining and furthering the demands of other psychologists that the traditional curricula be radically changed in accord with the principles of psychology. Besides de-emphasizing the study of the educational basics, he outlined what he considered to be the three main functions of the elementary school:

(1) to provide for each child six years of experience designed to enable him to make at each step in the period adjustments to the most essential phases of life... To adjust this general education to each child requires a considerable degree of specialization in accordance with individual differences. Consequently the elementary school has a second function, namely (2) to determine as accurately as possible the native intellectual capacities, the physical, emotional, temperamental, recreational,

8. *Ibid.*, 311-12.

aesthetic, and other aptitudes of children. Since
some pupils will find it necessary or advisable
to enter a vocation in the middle teens, a third
function is essential in some degree, namely,
(3) to explore the vocational interests and apti-
tudes of pupils and to provide some measure of
vocational adjustment for those who will leave
school at the earliest legal age.[9]

Let's look at each of these three main functions. We have spoken about Thorndike's views on
adjustment, on education as experience rather than
as the development of skills that access abilities
and individuality. The child, much like the animal,
is what he has experienced, tempered by the type
and condition of his brain and nervous system. If
his nervous system is in good order, then the child
will be able to respond properly to the stimuli to
which he is exposed. It is, of course, in the child's
earliest years that the nature of the stimuli is most
important, as these will most influence his character and personality.

Despite the careful control of stimuli and the
conditioning of behavior, however, something
might still go wrong. With all stimuli theoreti-
cally the same for a group of children, the con-

9. *Ibid.*, 310.

tinued difference in individual learning rates and abilities would indicate something physiologically different between youngsters. Hence, Thorndike's second point; psychological testing is used to determine just what the differences are. Testing each child regularly and thoroughly, in this view, allows one to determine individual learning disabilities or deficiencies. Thorndike's premise here is that intelligence is permanently set before the student enters school.[10] It is an easy conclusion, and it absolves educators from the responsibility for any of their students not learning, for if half the students in a classroom learn, that is proof enough that the teacher is teaching correctly. That the other half doesn't learn is obviously not the teacher's fault, as this half heard what the first half heard, and experienced the same stimuli. There must be something wrong with the second half, and psychological tests will determine what it is. Before 1900, the way to identify a good teacher was to determine that his students, at the end of their studies, knew a subject. With the emergence of psychological testing, however, teaching standards became dependent upon variables inherent in the nervous systems of the children, and thus out of the control of the teacher.

10. *Ibid.*, chapters X, XIII, *passim.*

The failure of many children to learn brings us to Thorndike's third point. He concluded that some students just won't make it, and that it's better to determine through educational testing who they will be, early enough so that they can be shunted into useful vocational training.[11] Here, Thorndike reflects, once again, a synthesis of the revised psychology of Wundt and the soft socialism of Dewey:

> *When all facts are taken into account, we believe it will be found that the best interests of the individual and society will be served by providing a certain number of the pupils least gifted in intelligence with the equipment*

11. Thorndike's rationale for vocational discrimination and selection through testing, as expressed in his many writings on the subject, was to provide the theoretical basis for yet another kind of discrimination. From 1913 on, psychologist H.H. Goddard (inventor of the term "moron") used psychological testing to "prove" the feeble-mindedness of great numbers of Jews, Italians, Hungarians, Russians and other Eastern Europeans attempting to immigrate to America through New York's Ellis Island, thereby forcing them to leave the country they had sacrificed so much to reach and return to Europe in time for the devastation of World War I. In the years before America shut its doors to vast numbers of immigrants in 1921, a new xenophobia was fueled by psychologists Louis Terman and Robert Yerkes, among others, who used psychological testing to "prove" the "racial dullness" of the Spanish-Indians and Mexican families of the Southwest and the general "feeblemindedness" of the "colored race." The social effects of the false racial ideas, massive sterilization campaigns, and other brutal eugenics measures spawned by the psychological testing movement are still with us.

needed to begin their vocational career by the completion of the junior high school period or even earlier in a few cases. Other individuals will advance their own welfare and that of society by securing but one more year, others by two, others by three additional years. Thus although the great majority of children should spend some time in the junior high school, not all of them should be expected to continue to the completion of the senior-high-school course. Each child should have as much high-school work as the common good requires.[12]

In summary, a German experimental psychologist was convinced that men are animals who can be understood by analyzing what they experience. His conclusions and methods were imported into an expanding American educational system and disseminated throughout that system to teachers, counselors, and administrators. Within half a century juvenile delinquency would run rampant, illiterates would pour out of the schools, teachers would no longer learn how to teach, and generation after generation of adults, themselves cheated out of the fruits of a good education, would despair of any solution to the morass of "modern" education.

---

12. Thorndike and Gates, *op. cit.*, 320.

5. A Gift From God

It took hundreds of millions of dollars to turn American education around in that short a period of time. Where did the money that inflamed this epidemic come from? How was it spent? How did the mainstream of experimental psychology meet up with a mainstream of millions of dollars?

The answer, it must be admitted, is enough to make one feel distinctly uneasy. The new psychology tapped the richest existing vein of American wealth and philanthropy and, in short order, won for itself the backing of almost unlimited funds. Here were its new buildings, its endowments, its publications, its research facilities, transportation, salaries—the wherewithal to spread like wildfire throughout the entire fabric of American education.

The checks were to emanate not from the uptown headquarters of Columbia Teachers College in New York City's Morningside Heights, but from No. 26 Broadway, around the corner from the financial capitol of the world on Wall Street.

No. 26 Broadway was the most famous business address in the country, perhaps in the world. It was the corporate home of the Standard Oil Company, owned and operated by John D. Rockefeller, Sr. The story of how the resources of the great oil monopoly came to be used in the spread of a new psychology covers a period of some 40 years, and begins with Mr. Rockefeller himself.

As every school child used to know, Rockefeller created one of the largest monopolies of his time. He began in the oil business in 1863, and by 1880 had won control of 95% of U.S. oil production. He controlled the drilling for oil, the refineries, the prices, and the transportation of crude and refined oil through an intricate tank car system. He sabotaged his competitors, hired spies to infiltrate the businesses of his enemies, and squeezed out independent operators by carefully conceived secret contracts. By 1910, when a glass of beer cost a penny and a loaf of bread less than a nickel, when a three-room apartment went for five dollars a month and a good pair of shoes for a dollar, Rockefeller had assets of over $800 *million* (in 1980's buying power, that equates to over $10 *billion*).[1]

---

1. The story of John D. Rockefeller's rise to wealth is related in Rockefeller family biographer and apologist Allan Nevins' *Study in Power: John D. Rockefeller, Industrialist and Philanthropist*, 2 vols. (New York: Charles Scribner's Sons, 1953).

Rockefeller liked to make money. At age 41, he was quoted as saying, "I have ways of making money you know nothing of,"[2] and later attributed his money-making powers to a gift from God:

I believe the power to make money is a gift from God–just as are the instincts for art, music, literature, the doctor 's talent, yours– to be developed and used to the best of our ability for the good of mankind. Having been endowed with the gift I possess, I believe it is my duty to make money and still more money and to use the money I make for the good of my fellow-man according to the dictates of my conscience. [3]

And make money he did but, his conscience notwithstanding, he became one of the most hated men in the country:

It was more than thirty years since he had begun his career, and Rockefeller was the central figure of the most spectacular suc- cess story in business history. The Standard

2. Abels, Jules, *The Rockefeller Billions: The Story of the World's Most Stupendous Fortune* (New York: Macmillan, 1965), 114-15.

3. *Ibid.*, 280.

was indisputably the most powerful industrial organization in the nation, and the most visible symbol of growing American might abroad. But for Rockefeller personally the price had been heavy: he had become identified with all the excesses the Standard had committed in its rise to power; hatred clung to him like iron filings to a magnet... Rockefeller had pursued his leviathan with complete dedication. But now he found himself lashed to its back as inextricably as Ahab, and in equal danger of being taken down for good.[4]

Rockefeller was excoriated by the organs of public opinion, and was the target of numerous investigating committees. His fortune and holdings were growing faster than he could control or protect them. He needed a special assistant who could both polish up his public image and act as hatchetman in the consolidation of his far-flung business empire.

Rockefeller, a Baptist, had over the years given sums of money to various Baptist causes. By the late 1880's, the church elders felt bold enough to ask Rockefeller to contribute to the rebuilding of the University of Chicago, a Baptist school

---

4.   Collier, Peter, and David Horowitz, *The Rockefellers: An American Dynasty* (New York: New American Library, 1976), 41.

founded in 1856 as the Morgan Park Theological Seminary. Acceding to their request, Rockefeller became immersed in the reconstruction of the university, giving to it in 1887 the then-huge sum of $600,000. It was during this involvement with the university that he met Frederick Taylor Gates, a Baptist minister who had previously worked for George A. Pillsbury, founder of the flour empire, in distributing Pillsbury's last philanthropies before his death.[5]

Rockefeller was impressed by Gates' directness and by the manner in which he handled financial affairs. Constantly besieged by requests for money, Rockefeller asked Gates to work for him and take the burden of philanthropic decisions off his shoulders. Gates was soon handling all requests for Rockefeller money, and doing what he could to polish up the Rockefeller image. He also reorganized Rockefeller's ownership of the great Masabi ore deposits in Minnesota (which provided 60% of the nation's iron ore), buying out the stockholders of personal holdings which were in trouble, and eliminating unprofitable holdings from the Rockefeller portfolio.

Gates grew frantic, however, at the extent of Rockefeller's financial holdings, and of the threat

5. *Ibid.*, 49-50.

they contained for Rockefeller: "Your fortune is rolling up, rolling up like an avalanche! You must distribute it faster than it grows! If you do not, it will crush you, and your children, and your children's children."[6] As Gates later recalled:

> *I trembled as I witnessed the unreasoning popular resentment at Mr. Rockefeller's riches, to the mass of people, a national menace. It was not, however, the unreasoning public prejudice of his vast fortune that chiefly troubled me. Was it to be handed on to posterity as other great fortunes have been handed down by their possessors, with scandalous results to their descendants and powerful tendencies to social demoralization? I saw no other course but for Mr. Rockefeller and his son to form a series of great corporate philanthropies for forwarding civilization in all its elements in this land and all lands; philanthropies, if possible, limitless in time and amount, broad in scope, and self-perpetuating.*[7]

6. *Ibid.*, 59.

7. *Ibid.*

6. Molding Hands

IF large philanthropy was to be the solution then there was only one way for the great monopolist Rockefeller to go about what he called "the difficult art of giving":

If a combination to do business is effective in saving waste and in getting better results, why is not combination far more important in philanthropic work?[1]

The game plan was simple: here was all this Rockefeller money, and here was Mr. Rockefeller being constantly badgered, scrutinized, and hauled into court; why not set up a monopoly on philanthropy, funnel into it large sums from the fortunes of Rockefeller and the other industrial barons, and distribute the money in a way guaranteed to ensure Mr. Rockefeller the respect and admiration

1. Rockefeller, John D., *Random Reminiscences of Men and Events* (Toronto: McClannand & Goodchild, 1909), 165.

of those elements of society which had castigated him most? In other words, it was time to launder the money.

The creation and funding of the University of Chicago had done much to enhance Rockefeller's public relations profile among Baptists and educators. Educational philanthropy, since it was paying off in good publicity, might be the way to go. The only difficulty was that education, on the whole, wasn't in bad shape. The indigenous American educational system was deeply rooted in the beliefs and practices of the Puritan Fathers, the Quakers, the early American patriots and philosophers. Jefferson had maintained that in order to preserve liberty in the new nation, it was essential that its citizenry be educated, whatever their income. Throughout the country, schools were established almost immediately after the colonization of new areas. Fine school systems were established by the Quakers in Pennsylvania and the Midwest. The free school movement in New York, under the aegis of DeWitt Clinton and Horace Mann, was flourishing. A large number of "normal schools" (so-called due to their role in setting the norms and standards of education) turned out thousands of well-trained teachers each year. Major universities had been established early in the country's history, and yearly graduated intensely literate and well-educated people who were to be the leaders of our nation.[2]

Educational results far exceeded those of modern schools. One has only to read old debates in the Congressional Record or scan the books published in the 1800's to realize that our ancestors of a century ago commanded a use of the language far superior to our own. Students learned how to read not comic books, but the essays of Burke, Webster, Lincoln, Horace, Cicero. Their difficulties with grammar were overcome long before they graduated from school, and any review of a typical elementary school arithmetic textbook printed before 1910 shows dramatically that students were learning mathematical skills that few of our current high school graduates know anything about. The high school graduate of 1900 was an educated person, fluent in his language, history, and culture, possessing the skills he needed in order to succeed.

Except in the rural South. The South had been devastated by the Civil War, and was undergoing

2. For an excellent description of education in New York at the turn of the century, see Palmer, A. Emerson, *The New York Public School: Being a History of Free Education in the City of New York* (New York: Macmillan, 1905). Sources of information about education in this country before the growth of the new psychology are scarce; much, however, was written critically about education once Columbia Teachers College was established. For an overview of the philosophical background to American education, see Vassar, Rena L., ed., *Social History of American Education*, 2 vols. (Chicago: Rand McNally & Co., 1965).

a period of reconstruction which broadly shifted traditional values and institutions. Few schools existed in rural areas, even for the white children, much less for the children of parents recently freed from slavery. It was in this rural South that Gates found the right circumstances for the implementation of his plans.

Some work had already been done in the reconstruction and development of the rural Southern educational system. The Peabody and Slater Funds had long been active in funding black schools, and the Tuskegee and Hampton Institutes were offering black children the benefits of industrial education, suitable for their future jobs in industry and agriculture.[3] One of the leaders in Southern

---

3. The Peabody Fund was the philanthropic brainchild of George Peabody, an American merchant who, in 1837, had emigrated to London and there founded a banking and brokerage house in partnership with another American, Junius S. Morgan. George Peabody & Co. did extremely well, even by British banking standards (Rothschild, Baring, etc.). J.S. Morgan's son , J.P., became the firm's New York agent. When Peabody retired, the firm became J.S. Morgan & Co. (1864), with headquarters in London. On the death of old J.S. in 1890, the son, J.P. Morgan, took over the firm and removed the headquarters to New York, naming the American office J.P. Morgan & Co. In 1883, however, George Peabody's son, the Rev. Endicott Peabody, co-founded and became first headmaster of Groton Academy, the prototypical anglophile prep school for America's aristocracy, and a leader in educational trends. J.P. Morgan was one of Groton's first trustees.

    The John F. Slater Fund ($1,000,000) was established in 1882 by the nephew of Samuel Slater, a British industrialist who came to America in 1789 to manufacture cotton machinery and came to be widely regarded as the founder of the American cotton industry.

education was Robert C. Ogden, a Northern merchant (manager of Wanamaker stores) who had assisted in the creation of Hampton Institute. Concerned about the condition of rural education in the South, he initiated a series of yearly education conferences and, in 1901, hired a train to take 50 prominent men and women on a grand tour of the schools of the South.[4]

John D. Rockefeller, Jr., who had worked at No. 26 Broadway for four years, saw the potential here and went along. On his return, Junior met with Gates to propose that his father's philanthropy be directed toward Southern education. He also discussed the idea with his father, and with the secretary of the Baptist Home Mission Society, Dr. Wallace Buttrick, a man who would wield considerable influence in education in the coming years.

John D. Rockefeller, Jr. played a central role in the Gates-Rockefeller connection. As he put it:

4. See Raymond B. Fosdick's memorial history of the General Education Board and Rockefeller philanthropy in education, *Adventure in Giving: The Story of the General Education Board, A Foundation Established by John D. Rockefeller* (New York: Harper & Row, 1962), *passim*. Keep in mind that the altruistic tone of Fosdick's tale is a public relations tool: this is the same Raymond Fosdick who, on JDR Jr.'s behalf, founded the eugenics-promoting Bureau of Social Hygiene and the government-restructuring Institute for Government Research (now part of the Brookings Institution), and who took over the International Association of Chiefs of Police in 1923 while overseeing the formation of Interpol (which was soon to be turned over to the Nazis and was, as late as 1972, directed by former SS officer Paul Dickopf).

Gates was the brilliant dreamer and creator. I was the salesman—the go-between with father at the opportune moment. Gates and I were father's lieutenants, each of us with a different task, but acting in perfect harmony. Gates did the heavy thinking, and my part was to sell his ideas to father. Of course, I was in a unique position. I could talk with father at the strategic moment. It might be in a relaxed mood after dinner, or while we were driving together. Consequently I could often get his approval of ideas which others couldn't have secured because the moment wasn't right.[5]

The younger Rockefeller was captivated by the possibilities of a Negro Education Board. After preliminary discussions, however, he decided not to limit the educational "philanthropy" program to one race.[6] Thus, at a dinner party on January 15, 1902, Junior laid out his plans to an assembled group of noted Southern educators, and received an enthusiastic response. A month later, the same group assembled again, this time to charter a new organization called the General Education Board,

5. *Ibid.*, 6.

6. It is also likely that both Rockefellers had, at this point, read Andrew Carnegie's *Gospel of Wealth*, published the previous year; enlightened paternalism was in the air.

for "the promotion of education within the United States without distinction of race, sex, or creed."[7] It was to be a philanthropic monopoly. In the words of Gates:

> *The object of this Association is to provide a vehicle through which capitalists of the North who sincerely desire to assist in the great work of Southern education may act with assurance that their money will be wisely used.*[8]

The new organization, after an initial donation by Rockefeller, Sr. of over $1 million, quickly absorbed the major existing philanthropic groups working in the South–the Slater and Peabody Funds. The General Education Board first assisted Robert Ogden's Southern Education Board, established several years earlier, then broadened its horizons to include other aspects of education. The real motivation behind the General Education Board, however, was perhaps best expressed in the Board's *Occasional Letter No. 1*, written by Gates:

> *In our dreams, we have limitless resources and the people yield themselves with perfect*

7. Ibid., 8.
8. Ibid., 9.

docility to our molding hands. The present education conventions fade from their minds, and unhampered by tradition, we work our own good will upon a grateful and responsive rural folk. We shall not try to make these people or any of their children into philosophers or men of learning, or men of science. We have not to raise up from among them authors, editors, poets or men of letters. We shall not search for embryo great artists, painters, musicians nor lawyers, doctors, preachers, politicians, statesmen, of whom we have an ample supply.

The task we set before ourselves is very simple as well as a very beautiful one, to train these people as we find them to a perfectly ideal life just where they are. So we will organize our children and teach them to do in a perfect way the things their fathers and mothers are doing in an imperfect way, in the homes, in the shops and on the farm.[9]

---

9. Gates also had strong views about fund-raising. Once, when asked about the feasibility of getting repeated donations from alumni he advised that people, having given once, were "more likely to give again when they could afford to. 'People bleed more easily after a vein has been opened,' he remarked." (According to Fosdick, *op. cit.*, 135.)

A similar view of the power of philanthropy was expressed by Board trustee Walter Hines Page (later to become editor of the Atlantic Monthly, ambassador to Great Britain, and early advocate of America's entry into World War I) to the first executive secretary of the Board, Wallace Buttrick:

> *...the world lies before us. It'll not be the same world when we get done with it that it was before: bet your last penny on that will you!*[10]

John D. Rockefeller, Sr.'s attention, however, was not just on grandly paternalistic schemes of social control. McClure's Magazine had begun publication of its serialization of Ida Tarbell's muckraking book, The History of the Standard Oil Company. Rockefeller was being hounded each day by hundreds of letters demanding or pleading for money, while the newspapers and magazines constantly attacked him and his organization.

> *Under the accumulating pressures, the body that he had pushed so remorselessly for the past forty years finally rebelled. Letters between Rockefeller and his wife during this period tell of sleepless nights. He began to suffer from*

10. Fosdick, op. cit., 12.

*serious digestive disorders, and his doctor
insisted that he retreat from his cares...
almost overnight the people who visited
Rockefeller came away shocked by his stooped
and careworn demeanor... His face had become
deeply lined; he had put on weight, sagging at
the midsection. He was ravaged by a nervous
disease...which left him without any hair on
his body, and in the first noticeable vanity of
an otherwise spartan life, he began to worry
about his baldness, hiding it first with a
grotesque black skull cap and later with a
series of ill-fitting white wigs, each of them
a slightly different length so that he could
imitate a natural growth of hair over a two-
week period.*[11]

Rockefeller's greatest desire at this time was
to buffer himself against his enemies and against
public opinion by pouring millions into whatever
medical or educational charities Gates could find.
He had enthroned Gates as his financial overseer,
and had increasingly turned over the job of laun-
dering his wealth to his son, John D. Rockefeller,
Jr., who over the years would seek out larger and
more effective ways of investing the Rockefeller

11. Collier and Horowitz, *op. cit.*, 45.

fortune toward, in Fosdick's words, "this goal of social control." These men, it can safely be said, conspired to control American education while buttressing the Rockefeller fortune against all attacks, ensuring that their autocratic views would prevail. With the General Education Board, Rockefeller's "education trust," a virtually unlimited source of funds was to be made available to the Wundtian psychologists' ambitious designs on American education.

7. Round Numbers

THE first contact between the two forces occurred during the height of anti-Rockefeller publicity in 1902:

> *Hardly had Dr. Buttrick opened his two-room office on Nassau Street in 1902 when a request came from Dr. James E. Russell, dean of Columbia University's Teachers College, and there was a note of urgency about it. The morning's mail had already brought in two letters from the South, Russell explained, and each day would bring in more–all from teachers seeking scholarship aid so that they might come North to complete their professional training... The General Education Board acted promptly, and within a few weeks scholarships of $300 each had been awarded to six normal school teachers in the South.*[1]

1. Fosdick, *op. cit.*, 298-99.

The innocent precedent was set, and the game was on. Teachers College needed money in order to accommodate its growing enrollment, expand its curriculum, and "influence American education, in accord with and even beyond its ambitions."[2] Dean Russell was to find his base of funding in the Rockefeller fortune, as expressed in this letter from John, Jr., to Russell in late 1902:

> *As a thank offering to Almighty God for the preservation of his family and household on the occasion of the destruction by fire of his country home at Pocantico Hills, New York, on the night of Sept. 17, 1902, my Father makes the following pledge:*
>
> *Understanding that the total indebtedness of Teachers College at the present time amounts to $200,000 in round numbers, which same was incurred partly because of a deficit in last year's running expenses, and partly by reason of certain necessary repairs and alterations; as soon as he shall receive satisfactory evidence that this entire indebtedness had been wiped out my Father will contribute two hundred and fifty thousand dollars ($250,000) as an endowment for the College.*

2. Joncich, *op. cit.*, 189.

Furthermore, during a period of two years from that date, my Father will duplicate, dollar for dollar, all contributions in cash made by others toward endowment, up to a total from him of two hundred and fifty thousand dollars ($250,000)...[3]

As a result, Teachers College experienced a "meteoric rise":

Only fifteen years after the move to 120th Street, Teachers College will meet the Rockefeller endowment terms and cover an entire city block crammed with seven buildings. Its facilities will operate from early morning to ten o'clock in the evening, for ten months of the year... Its enrollment is to be exceeded in size by only ten universities in the entire United States; only Columbia, Harvard, and Chicago will have more students seeking advanced education in 1912 as, amazingly, Teachers College becomes the fourth largest graduate school in the nation.[4]

3. *Ibid.*, 189-90.
4. *Ibid.*, 190.

Thus Teachers College was able to expand at a time critical to its success and hard on the heels of a massive population increase among school-age children. The number of public school enrollments reflected this increase, rising from 9,900,000 in 1880 to 12,700,000 only ten years later, and continuing to rise rapidly thereafter. The number of colleges increased from 350 in 1880 to nearly 500 in 1900, with college enrollment doubling over the same period, and continuing to expand into the early years of the new century.[5] There was an urgent need for teachers, and Teachers College was now firmly established and ready to fill that need with a methodology most schools of education didn't have—"educational" psychology.

The year after Rockefeller's General Education Board had set Teachers College financially on its feet, Thorndike published the first volume of his masterwork, Educational Psychology. By 1904, he was entrenched as full professor and head of the new department of educational psychology at Teachers College. That same year, after a decade in Chicago experimenting with children, John Dewey joined the faculty of Columbia University as a member of the departments of philosophy and education, in a unique

5.   Cremin, et al., op. cit., 6.

position to influence advanced students in Teachers College.[6] With Russell, Cattell, Thorndike, and the other Wundtians, Dewey set the ball rolling for an amalgam of "educational" psychology and socialism. It became known as "Progressive Education" and, emanating from Columbia's Teachers College for the next half-century, it slowly but surely became commonplace in every school in the country.

6. *Ibid.*, 45-6.

8. A Showplace

To Dewey and Thorndike, the schoolroom was a "great laboratory" in which to do their research and refine "the modification of instincts and capabilities into habits and powers."[1] Yet there was no large laboratory school at Columbia, no institution filled with willing or unknowing subjects for the great psychological experiments of the Wundtians at Teachers College–not until 1917, that is, when an offer to establish such a laboratory school came from Abraham Flexner of the General Education Board.

Abraham Flexner was an able fund-raiser, an experienced educator, and an organizer who felt he had the solution to both the supposed failure of American education and to the need of the General Education Board to disburse the Rockefeller millions.[2] Educated at Johns Hopkins University and

---

1. *Ibid.*, 44.

2. Flexner's very readable autobiography, *I Remember*, he later brought up to date and reprinted under the title *Abraham Flexner: An Autobiography* (New York: Simon & Schuster, 1960).

the University of Berlin, he apparently had little contact with the Wundtian psychologists at each institution. Flexner's experience in education came from fifteen years of running his own preparatory school in Louisville, Kentucky, and from his studies in German and American education while a researcher at The Carnegie Foundation for the Advancement of Teaching, in New York City. In 1913, Flexner left the Carnegie Foundation and went to work for the General Education Board, first as assistant secretary for four years, then as secretary (principal executive officer) running the operations of the Board for eight years in partnership with its president, Wallace Buttrick.[3]

The resident intellectual and educator on the Board, Flexner's forte was in digesting large amounts of information and making them palatable to others: his specialty was education. While Rockefeller and his son wanted only the relative peace and tranquility of millions in the bank, divorced from the manner in which those millions had been gained and safe from governmental and public attacks, Flexner saw more clearly than any other how that money could be used to further Progressive Education in the United States.

3. In 1928, Flexner resigned from his position as a trustee of the General Education Board in order to devote all of his time to the establishment and operation of Princeton's Institute for Advanced Study, home of the atomic bomb.

The University of Leipzig, now in the German Democratic Republic. *Keystone Press Agency.*

A view of Russell Hall, Teachers College of Columbia University. *Teachers College Library, Special Collections, TCana Collection.*

Officers of the General Education Board in the early '20's. Abraham Flexner is fourth from the left. "In our dreams, we have limitless resources and the people yield themselves with perfect docility to our molding hands."

Photos of Gates, Rockefeller Sr., Rockefeller Jr., and group photo of General Education Board, in ADVENTURE IN GIVING by Raymond B. Fosdick Copyright ©1962 by Harper & Row, Inc.

John D. Rockefeller: "I believe the power to make money is a gift from God."

John D. Rockefeller, Jr.: "I was in a unique position.
I could talk with father at the strategic moment."

Frederick T. Gates, the Baptist minister: "...unhampered by tradition, we work our own good will upon a grateful and responsive rural folk."

Flexner's first impact on American education had taken the form of "Germanizing" American medical education. While at the Carnegie Foundation, Flexner was asked to do a major study of medical schools in the United States and Canada. In eighteen months, Flexner visited each of the 155 medical colleges in the U.S. and Canada.[4] He was appalled by conditions which he considered inexcusable when compared with the medical schools he had seen in Germany. Nonetheless, he did find several medical schools of which he approved, most notably his alma mater, Johns Hopkins, which he considered to be "the one bright spot, despite meager endowment and missing clinics."[5]

Support for the "modernization" of American medical colleges rapidly developed in the General Education Board, which was looking for ways to expand its philanthropy beyond the narrow band of assistance to rural Southern education. Carnegie, who had fostered the study initially, would have nothing to do with medical funding, as "the practical Scot could see no point in helping insti-

---

4. Flexner used the same method of whirlwind, firsthand observation in his grand tour of European red light districts, preparing his 1914 book, *Prostitution in Europe*.

5. Fosdick, *op. cit.*, 152.

tutions which had allowed themselves to get into so abysmal a situation."[6] But at the request of the Carnegie Foundation, Flexner took off again, this time to survey medical schools in England, Scotland, France, Germany, and Austria. It was while he was writing up his final report that Gates invited him to have lunch with him. Gates was strongly interested in German medicine, and was opposed to the traditional homeopathic medicine used by Rockefeller's personal physician, Dr. H.F. Bigger, with whom he often had heated arguments. In the short meeting, Gates asked Flexner what he would do if he had $1 million to work with in developing medical education in the United States. Flexner replied that he would give it to Johns Hopkins. Gates sent Flexner off to his alma mater with the agreement that if Flexner could make a convincing case for the donation, it would be given by the Board. It was several years before Flexner finally cashed in, securing a $1.5 million gift from the Board to the German-oriented Johns Hopkins University. That same year (1913), he left Carnegie and joined the Board to direct the allocation of

6. *Ibid.*, 153.

Rockefeller millions to the development of chemi-
cally oriented medicine in the United States.[7]

By the time Flexner joined the Board, his attack
on American medical education, which had been
front-page news across the country, had resulted in
the number of medical schools in the United States
dropping from 147 to 95.[8] Naturopathic medicine
was on the decline in this country, as it was proving
particularly unsusceptible to Rockefeller funding.
Over the years (until 1960), the General Education
Board would give a total of over $96 million[9]
to medical schools which, like Johns Hopkins,
disregarded naturopathy, homeopathy, and chiro-
practic in favor of medicine based on the use of
surgery and chemical drugs. The Board's sponsor-
ship of chemical medicine on the one hand and
psychology on the other would culminate in 1963
when a group of researchers at Johns Hopkins
developed the use of Ritalin to "treat" children
who were regarded as "troubled" or too active. The
effects of this merger of chemical medicine and
Wundtian psychology upon American education
are thoroughly documented in *The Myth of the*

---

7. The disparity between Rockefeller's funding of German medicine, and
   his own personal disdain for it, is ably described in Collier and Horowitz, *op. cit.*, 59-61. See also Abels, *op. cit.*, chapters 28-30, *passim*.

8. Fosdick, *loc. cit.*

9. *Ibid.*, 328.

Hyperactive Child, and Other Means of Child Control, by Divoky and Schrag.[10]

Flexner's second major contribution to the transformation of American education and society came in 1916, with his plan to create an experimental laboratory school, backed by Rockefeller money, which would be a showplace for the Progressive Education practices of Dewey and Thorndike. Flexner presented his views to the public in a short tract called "A Modern School."[11] In it, Flexner attacked traditional American education and proposed a sharp break with workable educational practices. His experimental school would eliminate the study of Latin and Greek. Literature and history would not be completely abolished, but new methods would be instituted for teaching these subjects, classical literature would be ignored, and formal English grammar would be dropped. Flexner wasn't just throwing out the baby with the bath water; he was blowing up the tub.

10. Schrag, Peter, and Diane Divoky, *The Myth of the Hyperactive Child & Other Means of Child Control* (New York: Random House, 1975). For a deeper account of the broad general effects of this type of merger, see Schrag's devastating *Mind Control* (New York: Pantheon, 1978).

11. Flexner, Abraham, "A Modern School," *Occasional Papers*, No. 3 (New York: General Education Board, 1916).

9. Favoring Breezes

FLEXNER'S proposals were hardly as radical as those being promoted by Dewey and the other Wundtians working in education, but Flexner's booklet, presented to the public as a General Education Board paper with the full weight of the Rockefeller millions behind it, produced an instantaneous and dramatic reaction across the nation. At a time when German U-boats were stalking English shipping in the North Atlantic preparatory to American participation in World War I, and the newspapers were full of European news, *The New York Times* devoted a major editorial to Flexner's proposal, terming it "radical and dangerous," and "subversive of a very great part of what we hold to be sound and worthy in our present system of training":

Unblushing materialism finds its crowning triumph in the theory of the modern school. In the whole plan there is not a spiritual thought, not an idea that rises above the need of finding money for the pocket and food for the belly… It is a matter of instant inquiry, for very sober consideration, whether the General Education Board, indeed, may not with the immense funds at its disposal be able to shape to its will practically all the institutions in which the youth of the country are trained.

If this experiment bears the expected fruit we shall see imposed upon the country a system of education born of the theories of one or two men, and replacing a system which has been the natural outgrowth of the American character and the needs of the American people… The plans of the General Education Board call for careful examination.[1]

The dam broke into a national outcry against the General Education Board and its attempts to control and alter American education. From the *New York Journal of Commerce*:

Instances can be given in abundance where the mere prospect of an immense gift has changed the whole current of a college administrator's

---

1. *The New York Times*, January 21, 1917, Section 7 & 8, p.2.

thought and made him trim his sails on an entirely new tack to catch the favoring breezes of prosperity.[2]

From the *Manufacturers' Record*, Baltimore, Maryland:

Control, through possession of the millions massed in the Educational Trust, of two or three or four times as many millions of dollars in education makes possible control of the machinery and the methods of education. It makes it possible for the central controlling body to determine the whole character of American education, the textbooks to be used, the aims to be emphasized. Operating through State, denominational, and individual systems of schools and colleges, it gives the financial controller power to impose upon its beneficiaries its own views, good or bad, and thereby to dominate public opinion in social, economic and political matters.[3]

From the *New Orleans Times-Democrat*:

2. *Congressional Record (Senate)*, February 8, 1917, 2834.
3. *Ibid.*

The case here is plainly stated. The fund which the General Education Board administers is largely provided by men whose interest in shaping public opinion upon certain matters of vital concern to society and to the State is very great. Whether their philanthropy serves as a cloak to attain the ends desired, or whether the plan is unselfishly conceived and the sinister influence unconsciously exerted, the effect is likely to be the same in the end.

The gifts are hedged about by restrictions and conditions, with the education board to name them and to see that they are complied with. Every college which shares in the largess poses as a supplicant, in a sense. Not only is its policy partially directed by the Board, but it is additionally influenced, wittingly or unwittingly, by the desires of its benefactors.[4]

The debate continued onto the floor of the United States Senate, with Senator Chamberlain of Oregon leading the attack on the General Education Board and publicizing the views of numerous well-known American educators, among them Bishop Warren A. Candler, the Chancellor of Emory University in Atlanta, Georgia:

4. *Ibid.*

With this financial power in its control, the general board is in position to do what no body in this country can at present even attempt. It can determine largely what institutions shall grow, and in some measure what shall stand still or decay. It can look over the territory of the Nation, note the places where there is a famine of learning, and start new educational plants of any species it chooses, or revive old ones. It can do in many ways what the Government does for education in France and Germany. Its power will be enormous; it seems as if it might be able to determine the character of American education. The funds it holds represent only a fraction of the amounts which it will control; by giving a sum to an institution on condition that the institution raise an equal or greater amount, it will be able to direct much larger amounts than it possesses.

As a mechanism for controlling academic opinion there had, perhaps, never been anything in the history of education that would compare with the board system of subsidizing learning...

...we owe something to our ancestors, who founded and maintained our older institutions of learning. We have no right to bind up the offerings which they laid upon the altar of

higher education in the enslaving conditions prescribed by the Rockefeller board for institutions to which it grants its humiliating doles.[5]

The specific point in question had been the "modern school" proposed by Flexner, but the debate had deepened into what was to be the last major American stand against Progressive Education. After 1917 the takeover was rapid and thorough.

Even before the noise began to die down, Flexner and Teachers College went ahead with their plans for a laboratory school. Flexner had wanted to call it "The Modern School" (from the title of his booklet), but the phrase was so disliked that he decided to name it the Lincoln School.[6] The General Education Board, following Flexner's urgings, agreed to supply funds for the establishment and operation of the Lincoln School, and to pay the salary of a director.

The school was established at a temporary location in midtown Manhattan. Then, in 1920, the Board purchased a site close to Teachers Col-

5. *Ibid.*, 2831-32.

6. For a discussion of the Lincoln School within the context of foundation funding of Progressive Education, see Wormser, Rene A., *Foundations: Their Power and Influence* (New York: Devin-Adair, 1958), specifically Chapter 5, "Foundations and Radicalism in Education," *passim.*

lege, and invested approximately $1.25 million in building and furnishing the new school.

> *After the Lincoln School had moved to its new building, Teachers College and the General Education Board had discussions about what was called 'permanent financing.' After formal requests for endowment from Dean Russell…the General Education Board granted to Teachers College $500,000 in 1926, $500,000 in 1927, and $2,000,000 in 1928.*[7]

Wundtian psychology and Rockefeller money were now combined in an institution whose goal "was the construction of new curricula and the development of new methods."[8] Next, textbooks were created. Standard teaching practices were revised, and a course of study organized on the principles developed at Teachers College by Thorndike and Dewey. Here was the full-fledged prototype.

More than a thousand educators visited the Lincoln School in the school year 1923-1924. John D. Rockefeller, Jr., sent four of his five sons to study at the Lincoln School, with results that could, perhaps, have been predicted had he read the works of Thorndike and Dewey:

7. Cremin, *et al.*, *op. cit.*, 230.

8. Fosdick, *op. cit.*, 219.

*...Laurance [Rockefeller] gives startling con-
firmation as to "Why Johnnie [sic] Can't
Read.' He says that the Lincoln School did not
teach him to read and write as he wishes he
now could. Nelson, today, admits that reading
for him is a 'slow and tortuous process' that
he does not enjoy doing but compells himself
to do. This is significant evidence in the debate
that has raged about modern educational
techniques.*[9]

As an experiment in education, the Lincoln
School proved a disappointment, and it did poorly
financially despite continued Rockefeller support
to the tune of $5 million.[10] Finally closed down by
Teachers College in 1946, it was replaced by the
Institute of School Experimentation, which carried
on the task of remodeling American education.

*The judgment of the Trustees and adminis-
tration in 1946 that the Institute of School
Experimentation would prove to be a most
effective instrument for experimenting in the
public schools has been amply justified by*

9.   Abels, *op. cit.*, 343.

10. *Ibid.*, 334.

the Institute's record. Closing the School and using the endowment's funds for the Institute has had the effect of increasing the number of the College's educational laboratories. Where once Teachers College had laboratory schools only on Morningside Heights, it now had them all over the nation, and they are public schools with typical public school populations.[11]

11. Cremin, *et al.*, *op. cit.*, 238.

.

10. A New Social Order

THE Lincoln School, despite its inability to teach its students how to read and write, created broad effects on American education. Discarding the traditional course of study, it developed the core curriculum and merged the study of history, geography, and civics into what it called the "social studies." To a generation of teachers and administrators educated at Teachers College, the Lincoln School was a model for the type of school they were to create back home. To thousands of visitors, it was a showplace for the new psychology and Progressive Education. For the Rockefeller forces, it was a demonstration of the humanitarian intentions behind the Rockefeller fortune. Yet it was not, however large, the sum of all the Progressive Education activities at Teachers College. Nor did it represent the thousands of ways in which a now affluent Teachers College was forwarding the steady overhaul of American education. There is little in the way of change in our educational system and our society to which the professors at Teachers College didn't apply themselves. Dewey's disciples Harold Rugg, George S. Counts, and William H. Kilpatrick provide good examples of where Wundtian psychology was taking the teachers of our teachers.[1]

In the words of Rugg:

...through the schools of the world we shall disseminate a new conception of government—one that will embrace all of the collective activities of men; one that will postulate the need for scientific control and operation of economic activities in the interests of all people.[2]

Rugg proposed that this could be accomplished in three ways:

First and foremost, the development of a new philosophy of life and education which will be fully appropriate to the new social order;

1. By 1925, Rugg and Counts were reporting over 1,000 schools, nationwide, engaged in curriculum revision aligned with the new methods, 300 of these cooperating actively with the NEA's Bureau of Research (26th *Yearbook* of the National Society for the Study of Education; Bloomington, 1926).

2. Stormer, John A., *None Dare Call It Treason* (Florissant, Mo.: Liberty Bell Press, 1964), 105

Second, the building of an adequate plan for the production of a new race of educational workers; Third, the making of new activities and materials for the curriculum.[3]

Counts went further, proposing that the schools themselves build that new social order:

Historic capitalism, with its deification of the principle of selfishness, its reliance upon the forces of competition, its placing of property above human rights, and its exaltation of the profit motive, will either have to be displaced altogether, or so radically changed in form and spirit that its identity will be completely lost... That the teachers should deliberately reach for power and then make the most of their conquest is my firm conviction. To the extent that they are permitted to fashion the curriculum and procedures of the school they will definitely and positively influence the social attitudes, ideals and behavior of the coming generation.[4]

Although Kilpatrick's views were similar, he is mentioned here not so much because of his advo-

3. *Ibid.*

4. *Ibid.*, 102-4. See also Counts, George S., *Dare the School Build a New Social Order?* (New York: John Day Co., 1932).

cacy of Marxism or the new psychology in education but because, in 1914, he published a vitriolic attack on the teaching methods of Maria Montessori. He argued. that Dr. Montessori's "emphasis on individuality precluded the social interaction stressed in American progressive theories":

> *He complained further that the teaching materials were not stimulating; that children learned to read, write and figure too early; and that any good elements in the method were already contained in Dr. Dewey's theories, which went beyond those of Dr. Montessori. Dr. Kilpatrick's book had such impact that by 1918 the Montessori method was seldom mentioned in the United States, although it flourished elsewhere.*[5]

The result of Kilpatrick's diatribe was the suppression of the Montessori method in American education for the next 50 years.

Thorndike, meanwhile, was arranging for the publication of new spellers, arithmetic books, dictionaries (in collaboration with Barnhart), and textbooks on education and educational testing. And the General Education Board continued to

5. Calkins, Carroll C., *The Story of America* (Pleasantville, N.Y.: Readers' Digest, Inc., 1975), 134.

fund Teachers College, as well as the Progressive Education Association, the National Education Association, and others to the tune of 324 million dollars.[6]

By 1953, Wundtian psychology had reached out from Teachers College into virtually every public school in the land:

> *The single most powerful educational force in the world is at 120th Street and Broadway in New York City. Your children's teachers go there for advanced training... With 100,000 alumni, TC has managed to seat about one-third of the presidents and deans now [1953] in office at accredited U.S. teacher training schools. Its graduates make up about 20 percent of all our public school teachers. Over a fourth of the superintendents of schools in the 168 U.S. cities with at least 50,000 population are TC-trained.*[7]

Today, Wundt is remembered only by psychologists. Gates, Flexner, Cattell, Russell, even Thorndike, are found only in texts written by their

6. Fosdick, *op. cit.*, 250-1; "Foundation Quits," *Arizona Daily Star*, February 12, 1966.

7. Cremin, *et al., op. cit.*, 269.

disciples. They may seem irrelevant to today's critical educational problems: drug abuse, illiteracy, criminality, lowered standards, lack of motivation and self-discipline, and all the rest. Pick up a freshman college psychology text and you may well find no mention of Wundt, or even Cattell. Try to find a dictionary published after 1920 which has an unadulterated definition of "psychology." Question those who went to school before 1917, and find out what it was like. Check out the early works and histories of psychology; verify the facts, the names, dates, locations and events. Looking further you will find that despite the increasing billions that the large foundations and, now, the federal government, pour into American education, the situation just keeps getting worse. Despite the millions spent every year on the apparent development of psychology, this field has yet to come up with one workable solution to the problems of education, many, if not most of which, it now appears to have created.

Psychology currently constitutes the principal philosophical underpinning of our educational and, consequently, of our cultural outlook. From its largely bestial precepts major decisions in all walks of life are now made, and anyone attempting to determine the causes of a deep and lengthy national malaise must take into account psychology's covert hegemony over the thought processes of the body politic, the body economic, and the body social. Institutionalized as "education," it has become our largest single public expenditure at local, state, and federal levels.

The idea that Man is an exclusively physiological entity conflicts daily with the promise of a way of life conceived for, and attainable only by, men of free will. This idea (that Man is a stimulus-response animal) and the methods it implies, has played a critical role in transforming The American Dream into a national nightmare. It has turned our homes, schools, offices, stores, and factories into the battlegrounds of World War III; the draftees drift from encounter to encounter, increasing numbers succumbing as neurotic mental and spiritual casualties. The greatest number of victims, however, is in the 5-16 year-old range, as roughly one-quarter of the population is recruited into the compulsory federal behavior clinics cosmetically known as schools.

Those willing to decide on the basis of their own experience and observations whether they (and their children) are animals or not, and who choose not to be, must begin now to openly repudiate psychology's stranglehold on our children's future and awaken their neighbors from the nightmare.

Research Notes

ALMOST all of the deleterious effects created in education over the past 200 years can be traced, ultimately, to the unhappy influence of Jean-Jacques Rousseau and the uses to which unscrupulous shapers of society have put his doctrines of Man's relative insignificance and subservience to the forces of "nature."

The modern twist contributed by Wundt and his associates and disciples was so effective in the subversion of the principles and practices of education that it has led us to focus in *The Leipzig Connection* on that particular scenario and its principal protagonists.

Other characters in the story include the Germanic predecessors and contemporaries of Wundtian psychology: Froebel and his *Universal German Education Institution* in 1816, which spawned the kindergarten movement in the U.S. via the work of William Torrey Harris (later U.S. Commissioner of Education) and Susan Blow in St. Louis; Fechner, whose *Elements of Psychophysics* (Leipzig, 1860) pioneered, however misguidedly, the new technology of Man as animal; Brentano's Viennese empirical psychology with its offspring of "gestalt" and "humanistic" psychologies as imported to this country by Wertheimer through New York's New School for Social Research; and Felix Adler's[1] Seligman-sponsored Society for Ethical Culture with its British branch, the Secular Education League, founded by Stanton Coit in 1907.

Wundt's later work (1900-1920) was devoted almost entirely to the 9-volume *Volkerpsychologie* (*Ethnic Psychology*, still untranslated in this country). In it he investigated, per Schultz,

> *...the various stages of mental development in mankind as manifested in language, art, myths, social customs, law, and morals. The implications of this work for psychology are of far greater significance than its content, for it*

1. Born in Germany, Adler graduated from Columbia in 1870 and became professor of political and social ethics there in 1902. It may be well to remember here that the name Columbia, which the university adopted during the revolution, was cosmetically designed to protect the institution from the wrath of patriotic objection to its original name: King's College. There is no indication that the philosophy or purpose changed to match the name (see footnote 4, below).

served to divide the new science of psychology into two parts, the experimental and the social.[2]

It is specious to de-emphasize, as does this author, the content of Wundt's masterwork in an effort to obfuscate the source of a dominant ideology, for in this work Wundt contended that,

> *...social forces play a major role in the development of the complicated higher mental processes.*[3]

This is a direct attack on the concept and methods forwarded by traditional humanist educators and philosophers, that creative thought influences the development of social forces.[4]

2. Schultz, *op. cit.*, p. 47.

3. *Ibid.*

4. Emerging aspirations to greater individual and social self determination were also thwarted, in the late 18th century and throughout the 19th century, by an awesome body of English pseudo-philosophy, psychology, and political economic theory. These aspirations, expressed through a plethora of technological innovations and new republican groupings, posed a serious economic and political threat to the ruling European oligarchs.

   John Stuart Mill, an early master of oligarchic public relations, is a good example. While writing *On Liberty*, Mill was actually in charge of all correspondence from India House (in London) to the East India Company representatives on location in India, and was administering that conglomerate's shipments to China of, at that point, over 10 million pounds of raw opium a year.

Special mention should also be made of the concept of educational reform per se, and its leading exponents in Europe and the U.S., especially Johann Heinrich Pestalozzi. This disciple of Rousseau and of the Swiss mystic radical and physiognomist Johann Kaspar Lavater, having (as Swiss leader of the Illuminati)[5] first devised a workable system of public instruction for downtrodden children, provided the impetus for Froebel, Herbart, Mme. deStael, and a host of others to spread the idea of mass education as a state-supported agency

Official U.S. education circles long ago adopted the "democratic" ideas of these British court philosophers (Godwin, Bentham, Mill, Ricardo, Smith, Spencer, Arnold, Malthus, *et al.*). These ideas, as supported by establishmentarian liberalism, have eroded the foundations of our constitutional republic, generally speaking, and have made a mockery of the federalist policies out of which the U.S. Constitution grew, and of the federalist efforts that, alone, accomplished its ratification. As a result, American education has become, ideologically, an indoctrination network for essentially unconstitutional principles which ultimately lead to a sacrificing of national sovereignty. Combined with a psychological methodology producing, alternately, apathy and violence, the implanting of these ideas in the minds of America's school graduates opens the door to the creation of an abject, manipulated and reactive population.

The bucolic 1841 Brook Farm commune in this country was the Transcendentalists' anglophile prototype for an American Rousseauvian (and, ultimately, psychological) school system. Nathaniel Hawthorne, a Brook Farm founder, was later rewarded with a U.S. consulship to Liverpool. Brook Farm members called themselves the Phalanx, this term later becoming one of the trademarks of international fascism.

For an elaboration on the effects of official British philosophy on American culture, see the works of Lyndon LaRouche generally, and *The Campaigner* magazine and *New Solidarity* newspaper (Campaigner Publications, Inc., 304 W. 58th St., NY, NY 10019).

5.   Quick, R.H., *Educational Reformers* (New York: E.L. Kellog, 1891).

for direct social control and manipulation. This concept was decisively furthered in our own country by the work of DeWitt Clinton, Horace Mann, Henry Barnard and, via her apprenticeship at London's Toynbee Hall, Jane Addams. In the hands of such reformers the "socialization" of the student became the senior purpose of education. It was, essentially, to this ideology of "socialization" that Wundt's psychophysical principles were wed.[6]

To find a ray of hope in the story of education in the western world one has to go earlier than the period chronicled here, to the achievements of the Czech theologian and educator John Amos Comenius (Jan Amos Komensky), and to the work of John Milton (*Tractate of Education*), both in the 17th century, or to our own time in which non-

---

6. Pestalozzi's ideas were first introduced to the U.S. by his disciple, Joseph Neef, on a grant from the millionaire Scotsman (later, American) and father of American geology, William Maclure. Maclure funded Robert Owen's New Harmony utopian commune to the tune of $150,000 and dreamed of having Neef spread Pestalozzianism throughout the country from the pilot program at New Harmony. Owen's career in this country is exemplary. The "father of British socialism" established New Harmony (Indiana) in 1825 and, following its failure and his return to Britain, his disciples Robert Dale Owen (son) and Frances Wright went on to found the Association for the Protection of Industry and for the Promotion of National Education (Fanny Wright Societies) and militate nationally for federal- and state-supported free and compulsory schooling. Robert Dale Owen was able to promote this idea more effectively in his later role as a U.S. congressman. It was Neef's version of Pestalozzianism that was carried by the Fanny Wright Societies into a successful national movement, albeit not exactly according to Maclure's plans.

psychological methods are once again emerging from the debris left by Rousseau's heirs.

Sanity and enlightenment were built into American education in the late 18th century by the likes of Benjamin Franklin or the Quaker settlers who established important schooling systems throughout the midwest. The seeds they and others planted produced a vast and advanced network of schools and teacher training institutions throughout the U.S. This network did not reach everyone and there were flaws, to be sure, but the foundations were in place for an unprecedentedly effective national education program. What the country needed was bold educational policy that built on those foundations–what it got was an ideological takeover.

Many arguments have been put forth to the effect that our country's educational problems are derived from the fact and extent of government involvement in our schools. This is a fallacy promoted by those who simply cannot perceive either the true source of the evil or the enormous good to which an awesomely powerful and wealthy organization can be put if only it is led by enlightened forces. The fault lies not in the structure (for it is obedient) but in the ideas held by those using it, for they are either poorly educated or ill-intentioned. George Washington and Benjamin Franklin could take America's educational systems as they stand and overnight turn them into the most powerful force ever known for the elevation of mankind. Had they had the resources available to our educational leaders today, the concepts they put into motion would never have been outflanked by so ethically impoverished a combine as that revealed by our current account.

The thinking of world leaders is monitored by their educations. Solutions to world problems are now being devised and implemented by people who are the products of an exponentially deteriorating educational system.

Two hallmarks of a failed educational system are: 1) its inability to produce people who can resolve the problems of education itself, and 2) its propensity for elevating to positions of power and authority people who will invent, advocate, and enforce bizarre and destructive solutions. These "solutions" attack the culture like a cancer and prompt those responsible to apply a kind of cultural chemotherapy, painfully staving off the agonizing consequences of their ineptitude until a new echelon of mediocrats has succeeded them.

Life without education becomes a progressive shrinking away from the most positive and exacting dreams of Man.

Humanity is ill-organized. Geographically fragmented, it is spiritually and mentally even more dispersed by an informational oligarchy enthralling the populations of Earth with its psychologically programmed media. This curtain of disinformation drawn over our lives makes any betterment appear inconsequential and futile; all progress is reduced to mere news and is quickly overwhelmed by a relentless tide of deterioration, alarm, and crisis.

Compulsory universal government psychotherapy is not education.

Miseducation of both our leaders and their constituents or subjects is at the root of all our difficulties. Earth is educationally disenfranchised by the innate schemings of a universal ignorance. Nothing short of a complete educational renaissance will serve.

Bibliography

Abels, Jules, *The Rockefeller Billions: The Story of the World's Most Stupendous Fortune* (New York: Macmillan, 1965).

Allen, Gary, "Hands Off Our Children!", *American Opinion*, XVIII, No.9 (October, 1975).

----. *The Rockefeller File* (Seal Beach, CA, '76 Press, 1976).

Bernstein, Richard J., *John Dewey* (New York: Washington Square, 1966).

Binder, Frederick M., *Education in the History of Western Civilization: Selected Readings* (London: Macmillan, 1970).

Boring, Edwin G., *A History of Experimental Psychology* (New York: Appleton-Century-Crofts, Inc., 1957).

Bowen, H. Courthope, *Froebel* (New York: Charles Scribner's Sons, 1911).

Brubacher, John S., *A History of the Problems of Education, 2nd ed.* (New York: McGraw-Hill, 1966).

Butler, Nicholas Murray, ed., *Education in the United States* (New York: American Book Company, 1910).

Collier, Peter and David Horowitz, *The Rockefellers: An American Dynasty* (New York: New American Library, 1976).

Cremin, Lawrence A., David A. Shannon, and Mary Evelyn Townsend, *A History of Teachers College Columbia University* (New York: Columbia University Press, 1954).

De Garmo, Charles, *Herbart and the Herbartians* (New York: Charles Scribner's Sons, 1912)

DePencier, Ida B., *The History of the Laboratory Schools, The University of Chicago, 1896-1965* (Chicago: Quadrangle, 1967).

Dewey, John, *How We Think* (Boston: D.C. Heath & Co., 1910).

----. *Schools of Tomorrow* (New York: E.P. Dutton, 1915).

Dickson, Paul, *Think Tanks* (New York: Atheneum, 1972).

Dunkel, Harold B., *Herbart and Education* (New York: Random, House, 1969).

Flesch, Rudolph. *Why Johnny Can't Read* (New York: Harper & Row, 1955).

Flexner, Abraham, "A Modern School", *Occasional Paper No. 3* (New York: General Education Board, 1916).

----. *The American College: A Criticism* (New York: The Century Company, 1908).

----. *Prostitution in Europe* (New York: The Century Company, 1920).

----. *Universities: American, English, German* (New York: Oxford University Press, 1930).

Fosdick, Raymond B., *Adventure in Giving: The Story of The General Education Board, A Foundation Established by John D. Rockefeller* (New York: Harper & Row, 1962).

----. *John D Rockefeller, Jr., A Portrait* (New York: Harper & Brothers, 1956).

The General Education Board (An Account of Its Activities, 1902-1914) (New York: General Education Board, 1915).

Goy, Michael J., *The Missing Dimension in World Affairs* (S. Pasadena: Emissary, 1976).

Gray, J. Stanley, *Psychological Foundations of Education* (New York: American Book Company, 1935).

Hanaford, Phebe A., *The Life of George Peabody* (Boston: B.B. Russell, 1870).

Hayes, Carlton J.H., *A Political and Social History of Modern Europe, Volume II*, 1815-1915 (New York: Macmillan, 1922).

Joncich, Geraldine, *The Sane Positivist: A Biography of Edward L. Thorndike* (Middletown: Wesleyan University Press, 1968).

Kalimtgis, Konstandinos, *et al.*, *Dope, Inc.: Britain's Opium War Against the U.S.* (New York: The New Benjamin Franklin House, 1978).

Kane, W., *An Essay Toward a History of Education* (Chicago: Loyola University Press, 1938).

Latham, Earl, ed., *John D. Rockefeller, Robber Baron or Industrial Statesman?* (Boston: D.C. Heath and Company, 1949).

Mayer, Frederick, ed., *Foundations of Contemporary Education*, 3 volumes (New Haven: College & University Press, 1966).

Monroe, Paul, *A Brief Course in the History of Education* (New York: Macmillan, 1927).

Moore, Ernest Carroll, *Fifty Years of American Education: A Sketch of the Progress of Education in the United States from 1867 to 1917* (Boston: Ginn and Company, 1917).

Murchison, Carl, ed., *A History of Psychology in Autobiography*, 3 volumes (New York: Russell & Russell, 1961).

Murphy, Gardner and Joseph K. Kovach, *Historical Introduction to Modern Psychology*, 6th edition (New York: Harcourt Brace & World, 1972).

The National Cyclopedia of American Biography (New York: James T. White and Co., 1933, 1942, 1948).

Nevins, Allan, *Study in Power: John D. Rockefeller, Industrialist and Philanthropist* (New York: Charles Scribner's Sons, 1953).

Palmer, A. Emerson, *The New York Public School: Being a History of Free Education in the City of New York* (New York: Macmillan, 1905).

Quick, R.H., *Educational Reformers* (New York: E.L. Kellog & Co., 1891).

Rockefeller, John D., *Random Reminiscences of Men and Events* (Toronto: McClelland & Goodchild, 1909).

Salisbury, Allen, *The Civil War and the American System* (New York: University Editions, 1978).

Schlesinger, Arthur M., Jr., *Orestes A. Brownson, A Pilgrim's Progress* (Boston: Little, Brown, 1939).

Schrag, Peter, *Mind Control* (New York: Pantheon Books, 1978).

----, and Diane Divoky, *The Myth of the Hyperactive Child & Other Means of Child Control* (New York: Pantheon Books, 1975).

Schultz, Duane P., *A History of Modern Psychology* (New York: Academic Press, 1969).

Shipley, Thorne, ed., *Classics in Psychology* (New York: Philosophical Library, 1961).

Snow, Louis Franklin, *The College Curriculum in the United States* (New York: Columbia University Teachers College, 1907).

Stormer, John A., *None Dare Call it Treason* (Florissant, Missouri: Liberty Bell Press, 1964).

Thayer, V.T., *The Role of the School in American Society* (New York: Dodd, Mead & Company, 1963).

Thomson, Robert, *The Pelican History of Psychology* (Baltimore: Penguin, 1968).

Thorndike, Edward L., *The Elements of Psychology* (New York: A.G. Seiler, 1915).

----, *The Principles of Teaching, Based on Psychology* (New York: A.G. Seiler, 1925).

----, "The Contribution of Psychology to Education," *Journal of Educational Psychology, I* (1910), 5-6.

----, and Arthur I. Gates, *Elementary Principles of Education* (New York: Macmillan, 1929).

UNESCO, *The International Bureau of Education in the Service of Educational Development* (Paris: UNESCO, 1979).

United States Senate, *Congressional Record, February 8, 1917*, 2827-2841.

Vassar, Rena L., ed., *Social History of American Education, Volume I: Colonial Times to 1860* (Chicago: Rand McNally, 1965).

Weir, Alice M., *And There's Tomorrow* (Hawthorne, CA: Christian Book Club of America, 1975).

Whalen, Doran, *Granite For God's House: The Life of Orestes Augustus Brownson* (New York: Sheed & Ward, 1941).

Wormser, Rene, *Foundations: Their Power and Influence* (New York: Devin-Adair, 1958).

Zusne, Leonard, *Names in the History of Psychology: A Biographical Sourcebook* (New York: John Wiley & Sons, 1975).

About the author:

Paolo Lionni was born in Switzerland in 1938 and was educated there, in Italy, and in the U.S. (Brandeis University). During his lifetime he served as art director of several national magazines and his drawings, poetry, essays, and translations have been published in Europe, the U.S., and Mexico. For the last 15 years of his life, he was very active in the field of education promoting an alternative to the educational philosophies described in *The Leipzig Connection*.